# Meet the Gears
# A Family of Engineers

Sparky Riggs

Meet the Gears...

Dad, Mom and their son,
Mike are all Engineers.

Sam, their daughter, is only eight.
She loves to learn and create.

What is an Engineer?

It's where Math, Science and Technology come into play.

Engineers use all of that knowledge to solve problems that people face every day.

It is still not very clear.
Can you give me an example of an engineer?

There are many different kinds
of Engineers.

Some of them build
computers, planes and cars.

Others build skyscrapers, robots and rockets that can go to Mars.

# What kind of Engineers are you, Mom and Mike?

I'm a Computer Engineer. I build a computer chip that goes into a phone.

The chip works like a brain behind the phone's display.

It controls the power, memory, sounds and other cool things you do on your phone every day!

Computer Engineers build lots of other things
that make products come alive...

like televisions, computers and robotic cars
that know how to drive.

Dirty water flows from our house to her plant to get treated.
It then flows through machines where it's filtered and heated.

After it's clean, the water can be used for things like watering a tree.
Or it might even end up out in the sea!

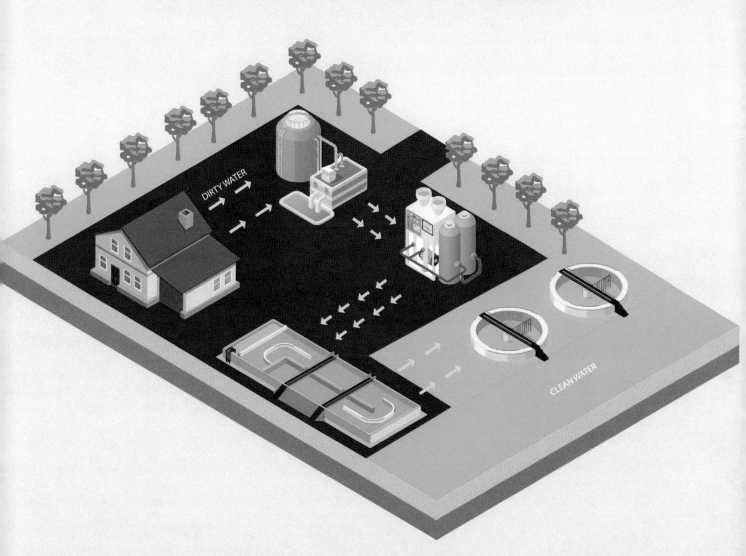

Your brother, Mike, is a Mechanical Engineer.

He works on building gas engines that move our cars on the road.

Some engines are built to go fast, while others
are built to carry a big load.

The engine mixes gas with airflow.
That combination is what causes the gears to go!

There are other kinds of engines being built by Mike's team.
Some use electricity and hydrogen gas, while others use steam.

Engine Pistons

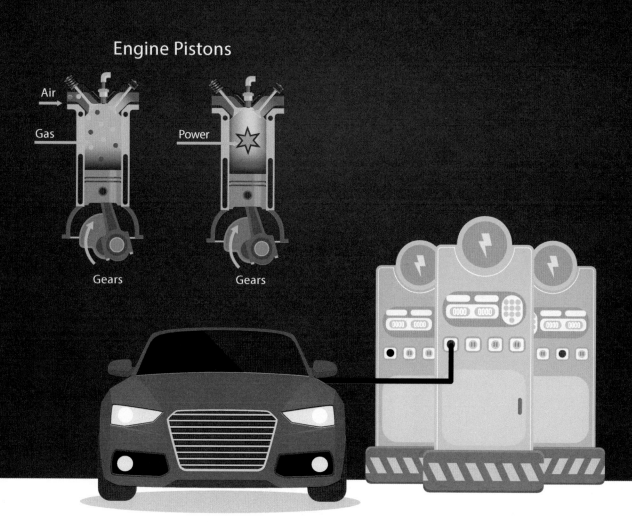

Air

Gas

Power

Gears

Gears

We also have other kinds of Engineers in your family tree.
Like Uncle Cole, Aunt Cassie and your cousins
Owen, Quinn, Fiona and Ashley

They are all very smart Engineers.
Some day they can tell you all about their careers.

Wow! Can I be an Engineer too someday?

Of course! As long as you have the will then there is a way!

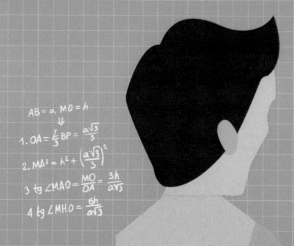

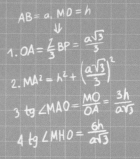

I love it Dad and I want to be an Engineer like all of you!
Tell me! Tell me! What do I need to do?

Yes! It all sounds very cool.
But to be an Engineer you have to study very hard in school.

An Engineering degree should remain at the core
And the best Engineers are always hungry to learn more!

But before we get too far into your future Engineering days.
Let's ensure your grades for Math and Science are straight A's

Along the way, you'll have plenty of problems to solve.
And
someday you'll be a great Engineer that will help the world evolve.

$AB = a, \ MO = h$

$\Downarrow$

$OA = \dfrac{\ell}{3} \ BP = \dfrac{a\sqrt{3}}{3}$

$MA^2 = h^2 + \left(\dfrac{a\sqrt{3}}{3}\right)^2$

$tg \angle MAO = \dfrac{MO}{OA} = \dfrac{3h}{a\sqrt{3}}$

$tg \angle MHO = \dfrac{6h}{a\sqrt{3}}$

$AB = a, \ MO = h$

$\Downarrow$

1. $OA = \dfrac{\ell}{3} \ BP = \dfrac{a\sqrt{3}}{3}$

2. $MA^2 = h^2 + \left(\dfrac{a\sqrt{3}}{3}\right)^2$

3. $tg \angle MAO = \dfrac{MO}{OA} = \dfrac{3h}{a\sqrt{3}}$

4. $tg \angle MHO = \dfrac{6h}{a\sqrt{3}}$

# To Be Continued...

$$\begin{cases} a = f(z) \\ \beta = f(z^2) \\ \gamma = f(z^3) \end{cases} \qquad \begin{cases} x = a^2 - \beta \\ y = 2\gamma \end{cases}$$

FOR THE ENGINEERS
THAT TURN DREAMS INTO REALITY

AND

FOR JENNIFER, COLE AND CASSANDRA

-SPARKY

Made in the USA
Monee, IL
22 October 2021